Library of
Davidson College

VOID

POLICY PAPERS IN
INTERNATIONAL AFFAIRS
*
NUMBER ONE

IMAGES OF DÉTENTE AND THE SOVIET POLITICAL ORDER

KENNETH JOWITT

INSTITUTE OF INTERNATIONAL STUDIES
UNIVERSITY OF CALIFORNIA
BERKELEY

In sponsoring the Policy Papers in International Affairs series, the Institute of International Studies reasserts its commitment to a vigorous policy debate by providing a forum for innovative approaches to important policy issues. The views expressed in each paper are those of the author only, and publication in this series does not constitute endorsement by the Institute.

The author would like to thank Gregory Grossman, Steven Krasner, and Robert Price for their critical comments.

International Standard Book Number 0-87725-501-6

© 1977 by the Regents of the University of California

CONTENTS

I. THE FUTURE OF STEREOTYPIC RELATIONS	1
II. KISSINGER'S IMAGE OF DETENTE	3
III. BRZEZINSKI'S IMAGE OF DETENTE	9
IV. BREZHNEV'S IMAGE OF DETENTE	12
V. EASTERN EUROPE, WESTERN EUROPE, AND DETENTE	21
VI. PROPOSED WESTERN POLICY CHANGES	24

I. THE FUTURE OF STEREOTYPIC RELATIONS

The political choices available to states in the international arena will depend more on the *type* of detente that exists between the United States and the Soviet Union than on anything else. In contrast to the cold-war setting, detente results from the entry[1] of the Soviet Union into the world arena and the end of a period of Soviet withdrawal and insulation from that same arena.[2] Detente also reflects a change in the United States' international position. Defeat in Vietnam and the emergence of Soviet global power have placed political, military, and economic limits on what American policy makers have perceived as an almost limitless international "frontier" for twenty years. What is at issue is how the United States and the Soviet Union are responding to these new global realities, how they may respond in future, and how such responses might affect the policies and relationships of other states.

Paradoxically, the prospects for limiting international conflict depend on America's capacity to deal with "Russia in terms of a world policy [rather than] dealing with the world in terms of a Russian policy,"[3] and on the Soviet ability to decouple its foreign policy from its domestic policy and problems. The paradox is that both these shifts must occur in the context of increasing Soviet power, a development that encourages the existing American practice of defining world policy in terms of Russian policy, and the Soviet practice of subordinating its foreign policies to its domestic policies. The issue is whether or to what extent detente will facilitate the

[1] By "entry" we refer to the continuous participation of the Soviet state in areas all over the world and the Soviet stake in regulating that participation in a way that favors the effective and stable defense of its interests.

[2] In a number of respects the problems faced by the Soviet regime as it enters the global international arena are comparable to those faced by the Soviet Party's "entry strategy" in its own society. For an analysis of the latter process see the author's "Inclusion and Mobilization in European Leninist Regimes," *World Politics*, Vol. XXVIII, October 1975, pp. 69-97.

[3] See Robert Tucker, "Russia, The West, and World Order," *The Soviet Political Mind* (New York: Praeger, 1963), p. 183.

IMAGES OF DETENTE AND THE SOVIET POLITICAL ORDER

replacement of a stereotyped international world order[4] based on rigid, hierarchical, and compartmentalized relations among states with one founded on a much greater degree of combinatorial freedom and political choice for states of all sizes. Images and strategies of detente can be compared and evaluated in terms of these two polar patterns of international order: one based on a stereotyping of political identities and choices, the other based on multiple rather than exclusive state identities and choices.

The cold war provides an instance of extreme stereotyping. One state in each camp patriarchally monopolized political decisions for the camp as a whole. The behavior of any member of either camp (Liberal or Leninist) could be predicted simply by knowing which camp it belonged to. Exceptions were rare and isolated—e.g., Yugoslavia in 1948 and France and England's Suez venture in 1956. Mutual fear of contamination was matched by mutual efforts at disrupting the other camp. The members of each camp were one-dimensional entities insofar as each defined itself in terms of only one membership, membership in its camp; one referent, the leader of their respective camps; and one identity, the ideology that formally distinguished the members of one camp from the other. Thus, entities as different as Albania and East Germany were viewed almost exclusively as communist, just as Norway and Italy were viewed one-dimensionally as free world countries.

The nineteenth century provides an historical instance of a world order based more on flexibility and diversification than on stereotyping of political organization and identity. In that setting a significant number of states had multiple identities and memberships available to them. At different times, or even at the same time, a state might define itself as a European state, a colonial power, a free trader, a member of a military coalition, and so on. The range of roles was limited, but for a number of states it was possible to choose a set of complementary memberships, policies, and roles rather than mutually exclusive ones.

Detente can be organized in more or less stereotypic terms, with individual states more or less categorically assigned a position in a hierarchically compartmentalized system that narrows the memberships, roles, and policies available to them. The greater the element of stereotyping in the organization of international relations—in other words the degree of bloc compartmentalization, centralized

---

[4]By "world order" we mean a discernible and regular pattern of leadership-membership definitions in international groupings. The range and character of such groupings determine the type of world order that exists.

leadership and, most critically, the narrowing of available political memberships—the greater the isolation, dependence, and political fragility of those lower in the hierarchy—i.e., the East European regimes. Finally, at a time when the two superpowers are relatively equal in military weight and are interacting continuously in a diverse set of arenas, attempts on their part to maintain a stereotyped pattern of international relations increases the likelihood of conflict.

These arguments can best be elaborated by examining the three most influential images of detente: those of Kissinger, Brzezinski, and Brezhnev.

II. KISSINGER'S IMAGE OF DETENTE

Kissinger's position appears to rest on two basic assumptions. First, he feels that the Soviet political order[5] is a seriously "faulted"[6] one, poorly integrated both domestically and internationally. In Kissinger's view the Soviet political order contains a set of structural problems that seriously challenge the power of the Soviet leadership to maintain stability. Second, he feels that because the Soviet leadership now possesses enormous nuclear power, the United States must *enmesh* the Soviet Union in a series of constraining commitments. In the event of a major breakdown in any sector of the Soviet political order, these commitments would, ideally, rule out a Soviet attempt to displace internal or bloc conflict

[5] In referring to the Soviet political order we have in mind *both* the Soviet Union and the Soviet hegemonic position over Eastern Europe.

[6] The term "fault" refers to institutional amalgams of antithetical principles. The stability of such an amalgam depends on the ability of leadership to offer rewards to representatives of opposing principles—e.g., the passing of laws favorable to landlords preventing peasants from moving to urban areas (to become industrial workers) and the passing of protective infant industry legislation to satisfy the claims of industrialists. Such a situation requires a great deal of disposable uncommitted resources in the system to allow for the payment of rewards that conflict with one another. In the absence of such resources a stable amalgamation of antithetical principles, such as claims to hegemony vs. claims to equality, secularism vs. religiosity, agricultural-feudal vs. industrial-capitalist policies, depends on the use of force. Fascism and imperialism are typical responses to such a situation. In the Soviet case a related development might take the form of a Russian ethnic-militarist leadership group coming to power. For an analysis of Imperial Germany based on the notion of a "faulted society," see Ralf Dahrendorf, *Society and Democracy in Germany* (Garden City, New York: Anchor Books, 1969), pp. 46-63.

on the international arena through acts of imperialism or war. For reasons of his own Brezhnev has adopted an overall strategy emphasizing economic considerations, and this strategy fits in with Kissinger's position very well. Both leaders prefer strategies that attempt to shift potentially dangerous political issues into an economic frame of reference, although this shifting does not deprive these issues of their political quality. For Kissinger such a shift has the added benefit that the United States is advantageously placed in any economic competition—a situation which Brezhnev's domestic critics are well aware of.

Kissinger wishes to combine a balance of power with a functionalist integrative strategy. American military and economic power are to be used to set up a reward and punishment schedule that will lead the Soviet Union into accepting a definition of competition with the West which would ideally achieve several things: (a) first and foremost, it would reduce the likelihood that the Soviet leadership could use war or imperialism to displace any crisis that might develop around one of the "faults" in the Soviet political order;[7] (b) it would allow the United States to sustain its *primus inter pares* status in its relations with Western Europe and the rest of the world; and (c) it would indirectly influence Eastern Europe so as to avoid the high risk of supporting nationalist challenges to Soviet hegemony in the area—challenges that can only heighten Soviet efforts at control.

Kissinger described his strategy of political-functional enmeshment to the Senate Foreign Relations Committee in these terms:

> Our approach proceeds from the conviction that in moving forward across a wide spectrum of negotiations, progress in one area adds momentum to progress in other areas. If we succeed, then no agreement stands alone as an isolated accomplishment vulnerable to the next crisis. . . . By acquiring a stake in this network of relationships with the West, the Soviet Union may become more conscious of what it would lose by a return to confrontation.[8]

This "molasses" strategy of raising the cost of confrontation through mutually beneficial commitments in as many areas as possible, of tying Soviet hands and limiting potentially rash actions, depends on strategic parity and a complex pattern of economic ties: ties between the United States and the Soviet Union, Western Europe and the

---

[7] These "faults" are examined in Section IV.

[8] See U.S. Department of State, Bureau of Public Affairs, Special Report No. 6, *Statement on U.S.-Soviet Relations, September 19, 1974* (Washington, D.C.: Government Printing Office, 1974), p. 5.

Soviet Union, the United States and Western Europe, the Soviet Union and Eastern Europe, and the United States and Eastern Europe. This web[9] should both stabilize and influence the evolution of the Soviet Union and Eastern Europe.

Sonnenfeldt's statement about Soviet-East European "organic unity" does *not* signify a shift in Kissinger's political and ideological opposition to Soviet and communist power. The premise for Sonnenfeldt's statement is one shared by a number of students of East Europe—including Brzezinski, one of Kissinger's critics. Brzezinski pointed out some ten years ago that indiscriminate support of East European nationalism was a two-edged sword.[10] Kissinger's East European policy is intended to defuse one of the basic "faults" in the Soviet international order: anti-Soviet nationalism, a force that could trigger World War III (a la World War I). Kissinger seems to realize that "bridge-building"—as Brzezinski's approach to detente was labeled—is a provocative and self-defeating exercise (for reasons that we shall shortly mention). But it is doubtful that Kissinger's indirect approach to Eastern Europe is likely to be any more successful in breaking the stereotypic patterns that the Soviet leadership is currently attempting to reinforce in that area.[11]

Kissinger hopes that proliferating economic and technological ties will create interests and ideologies in both the Soviet Union and Eastern Europe that will strategically influence the developmental pattern of Eastern Europe without directly challenging the Soviet Union politically or ideologically. Kissinger realizes that the Soviet Union must be our primary if not exclusive point of reference in dealing with Eastern Europe, particularly if we are to continue our claim to primacy in West European affairs.

[9] The most influential and elaborate statement of neofunctional integration is that developed by Ernst Haas. The appeal of this strategy is the promise it offers of achieving major political outcomes through non-political devices. Each of the three images of detente discussed here relies to some extent on what Haas has termed the "spillover effect." See Haas, *Beyond the Nation-State* (Stanford: Stanford University Press, 1964) and *Tangle of Hopes* (Englewood Cliffs, N.J.: Prentice-Hall, 1969).

[10] See Zbigniew Brzezinski, *Alternative to Partition* (New York: McGraw-Hill Book Co., 1965), in particular p. 137. This work makes a number of *premature* claims about ideological "erosion" in the Soviet Union, the return of international politics to Eastern Europe, and the likelihood of the Soviet Union accepting a social-democratic, Finland-like Eastern Europe.

[11] For a very useful discussion of Soviet efforts to standardize East European regimes, see J.F. Brown, "Detente and Soviet Policy in Eastern Europe," *Survey* (Spring/Summer 1974), pp. 46-59.

IMAGES OF DETENTE AND THE SOVIET POLITICAL ORDER

The Secretary of State has elaborated a sophisticated synthetic policy based on (a) an appreciation of Soviet military power and critical Soviet political weaknesses; (b) a desire to reduce the likelihood that, faced with an internal crisis (within the Soviet Union or the bloc), the Soviet leadership would consider externalizing the crisis through imperialism or war; (c) a desire to prevent Soviet strategy from isolating the United States from its West European allies; and (d) an attempt to influence East Europe primarily through multilateral ties with the Soviet Union. *This tilt towards the Soviet Union is based on the correct perception that although the Soviet political order has a high crisis-potential, it is an order with major stabilizing resources and devices, like the Imperial German Rechstaat it resembles in critical respects.*[12] *U.S. policy must be simultaneously sensitive to the crisis-potential and responsive to the elements of stability and power in the Soviet political order.* In Kissinger's view direct influence on the Soviet order supplemented by specific connections with individual East European regimes will be more likely than any other strategy to temper any possible political rashness in East Europe. It should also create a web of interests, commitments, constraints, and groups that will incrementally contribute to the *stable* evolution of East Europe (and the Soviet Union).[13] Given his own attitude about the United States' role in Latin America, Kissinger can appreciate Brezhnev's attitude towards East Europe, and from a practical point of view he realizes that the opportunities are too few and the dangers too great to attempt to influence and control directly the movement of that area towards the West.

There are at least two weaknesses in Kissinger's image of detente. To begin with, there is ample reason to assume that certain segments of the Soviet leadership oppose the Kissinger (Brezhnev) detente strategy. These individuals worry that detente will produce constraints on Soviet maneuverability just when Soviet power has

---

[12] This analogy is developed in an unpublished paper by the author (prepared for a Conference on Political and Social Development in Eastern Europe, at the University of California, June 1973), titled "State and National Development in East Europe."

[13] That both Kissinger and Brezhnev seek more stable relations between the United States and the Soviet Union is clear from their policy statements. They also agree on the meaning of stability. For both men, "stable" implies relations that are more regular, continuous, and calculable. Relations and interactions that are sporadic, disjointed, and incalculable are unstable. As the two global-nuclear powers come more frequently into contact, both leaders want to establish a pattern of international interaction based on shared executive conventions in place of *ad hoc* responses to events.

reached a new, dramatic point. Moreover, some members of the Soviet leadership feel that the emphasis on economic ties between the Soviet Union and the United States will lead to a new neocolonial status for the Soviet Union vis-a-vis Western technology, culture, and ideology. Given the existence of such views and groups in the Soviet regime, every new link between the United States and the Soviet Union increases the likelihood that these groups will do all they can to reverse the process. While it is impossible to measure accurately the relative power of competing groups or individuals in the Soviet regime, it is possible to argue that any new leadership could break any web that has thus far been woven and any that is likely to be woven in the near future. For example, if in the context of the Common Market, a DeGaulle with much less power and many more constraints was able partially to challenge the logic of increasing economic and political integration, there is no reason to assume that a Soviet leadership could not act in the same way. In fact, given their ideological-institutional concerns and substantial economic power, the Soviet leaders' ambivalence about mutual enmeshment must be at least as great as that evident among certain elements in the West who oppose Kissinger's policy.

However, there is a second and much more fundamental problem with Kissinger's image of detente than his overly hopeful view that because of mutual Soviet-American interest in avoiding high-risk and high-cost situations, enmeshment will at least reach critical thresholds in strategic problem areas. The major difficulty with Kissinger's image of detente is his commitment to a detente that is *indivisible*.[14] The combination of a Soviet political order that is seriously "faulted" and a Soviet-American detente that enmeshes the United States ever more directly into such a setting creates extremely high risks. By attempting to enmesh the two systems, Kissinger contributes to the potential scope and intensity of any crisis that originates along one of the several "faults" in the Soviet political order. A wiser course would be to establish more disaggregated sets of ties, a pattern of relations that would tend to isolate and decentralize individual crises. In light of Kissinger's presumed sensitivity to the stability-crisis potential that characterizes the Soviet political order, what explanation is there for such a risky attempt to enmesh the Soviet system in a set of mutual commitments with the United States? The answer lies in the fact that this strategy favors American control over the direction of developments with global consequences. *It is the continuing commitment to hierarchy and centralized con-*

---

[14] See *Statement on U.S.-Soviet Relations*, p. 6.

trol, the assumption that only through hierarchy and centralization can stability be assured, that explains the Kissinger "risk."

A conception of indivisible detente based on hierarchical and centralized control amounts to a major revision in the organization of the stereotyped world order, *not* its demise. Kissinger is an adaptive conservative, not a radical. His policy of detente is an attempt to *maintain* the central management of the two alliance systems in an international environment that has experienced a major change since 1970. His continued commitment to central-hierarchical command of the Western bloc and his expectation that Western obedience will follow American commands are reflected in his approach to the Portuguese revolution, the possibility of Italian communist participation in government, and the Angolan civil war. In each instance, Kissinger asserted the immediate and direct interest of the United States. In each instance, the role of regional or domestic actors (i.e., the Social Democratic parties of Western Europe, the Church and peasantry in Portugal, and internal factors in Angola) were relegated to secondary positions—though events in most cases subsequently demonstrated their primary weight.[15]

Kissinger and Brezhnev have each acted to maintain his respective state's dominant position while simultaneously seeking to prevent the other from acting rashly. The intent has been to enmesh each other in a pattern of relationships that will provide relative stability and allow for the gradual development of each one's system at the expense of the other. Unfortunately, it is more likely that indivisibility and central management will add to international instability even more than the cold-war combination of bloc compartmentalization and central management of alliance systems. In a world in which the number of articulation and organization points for conflict has expanded, hierarchy and a web of mutually constraining commitments amount to useful tactics but poor strategy. In both Kissinger's and Brezhnev's schemes, each plan's success depends on a continuously fragile displacement of political concerns by economic concerns in an effort to deal with what are increasingly political issues revolving around the notion of *equality*.

These issues are illustrated by the oil crisis, which was as much a demand by Arab states for political recognition and status as for economic equity. They are expressed in East Europe by arguments against a Soviet hegemony in the World Socialist System,[16] argu-

[15] Even in the Angolan case, Cuban action was more important than Soviet action and not thoroughly subordinated to it.

[16] "World Socialist System" refers to all ruling communist regimes.

ments made explicitly by the Romanians, Yugoslavs, and Albanians and enjoying a significant degree of acceptance in Hungary and Poland. They are expressed in West Europe not only by the French emphasis on sovereignty, but also in the refusal of various West European regimes to subordinate their specific interests to an undifferentiated American reference to the "interests of Western security." Reductions in the French and British defense outlays, the West European lack of response to American requests for transit points during the 1973 Arab-Israeli conflict, socio-political developments in Italy, Spain, and Portugal, and the Greek-Turkish conflict are instances and indicators of a significant, perhaps basic, revision in the "West European" region.

III. BRZEZINSKI'S IMAGE OF DETENTE

As an alternative to Secretary Kissinger's image of detente, Professor Brzezinski's is not very compelling—either analytically or politically. Brzezinski's approach to detente in the sixties was labeled "bridge-building." "Bridge-building" was then, and presumably remains, an assimilationist strategy. Eastern Europe is to become part of the West through a series of ties with Western Europe (especially with the Common Market). The Soviet Union would not see them as threatening because the West would give assurances that such ties were not linked to the restoration of capitalist economic organization in Eastern Europe or to any attempt at military advantage. The combination of multilateral economic ties and the shelving of discussion about liberalization were supposed to result in a social-democratic, "Finlandized" Eastern Europe.

The fundamental error underlying this concept and policy was Brzezinski's superficial treatment of ideology. In his view the Soviet Union and Eastern Europe have been undergoing something called ideological "erosion." In turn this process of erosion is directly related to the growth of state interests in Eastern Europe—i.e., state interests grow in zero-sum fashion at the expense of ideology. This schematic view allowed Brzezinski to argue that the development of a social-democratic, Finland-like Eastern Europe would be tolerated both by the Soviet elite and the communist elites of Eastern Europe.[17] Within the terms of Brzezinski's argument the only

---

[17] See *Alternative to Partition*, p. 48: "It is no longer beyond the realm of

barrier to such an evolution was ideology, and that was supposedly eroding. As more "pragmatic" state interests grew and as ideology eroded, no rational state actor including the Soviet Union would see the emergence of a social democratic Eastern Europe as a danger to its interests. In fact, Brzezinski (at least in 1965) noted that, at some point along the erosion continuum, East Germany might "eventually lose even its appeal as a buffer, and begin to resemble a Soviet Mozambique, a source . . . of embarrassment to Moscow."[18]

In fact, ideology is not coterminous with dogma (except by assertion or definition), nor is the development of ideology limited to a process of erosion. Erosion is one possible outcome; but institutionalization of ideology may also occur and has occurred in the Soviet political order. One place ideological erosion did *not* occur was within Brzezinski's image of "bridge-building." For all the claims about not challenging Soviet interests in the area (let alone the East European regimes' interests), "bridge-building" had as its goal the assimilation of these regimes to liberal forms. Another goal was the implicit isolation of the Soviet Union. This pattern of assimilation-isolation links Brzezinski's "bridge-building" and later Trilateral[19] concerns.

The Trilateral conception offers a more inclusive and flexible compartmentalization of the world than the Cold War conception. The West, with Japan now included, would coordinate its activities so as to prevent any political contamination and contain any challenge from the Soviet political order. Trilateralism would mean revitalization of the American bloc, continued efforts to assimilate Eastern Europe through Western European mediation, and isolation of the Soviet Union. Stanley Hoffman's comment rings true: that if Kissinger's inspiration is with the 1880's, Brzezinski's is with the 1950's.[20]

At one point in *Alternative to Partition,* Brzezinski noted that

possibility that in the course of the next decade or so the Soviet leaders will reluctantly conclude that their position in East Europe would be stronger if the East European states ceased to be unpopular and unstable dictatorships and came to resemble Finland."

[18]*Ibid.*, p. 140.

[19]"Trilateral" refers to the Trilateral Commission on which Brzezinski served as Director.

[20]Hoffman suggested that "Mr. Kennan's obsession was 1914, while Mr. Acheson's was 1938. Mr. Kissinger's inspiration remains the 1880's and Mr. Brzezinski's the 1950's." "Choices," *Foreign Policy*, Vol. 12 (Fall 1973), p. 18.

"detente inevitably challenges Soviet control over East Europe."[21] It is even more important that different types of detente challenge Soviet control in more or less subtle ways. "Bridge-building" and Trilateralism almost predictably produce two things Brzezinski says he wants to avoid—increased efforts by the Soviet leadership to standardize[22] and insulate East European states from the potentially contaminating effects of contact with West Europe and, in response to these efforts, sporadic anti-Soviet nationalist responses by East European regimes. Based on two somewhat superficially defined assumptions—that Soviet ideological change is coterminous with ideological erosion and that America is pragmatic, not ideological (instead of an amalgam of both)—Brzezinski's image of detente could only act as direct provocation to the Soviet and East European leaderships, and perhaps leave some Western proponents of "bridge-building" insensitive to the highly ideological, non-pragmatic bases of that strategy.

Brzezinski's images of detente do have certain strengths. They avoid the dangers implicit in Kissinger's emphasis on the indivisibility of detente. But in place of *indivisibility* Brzezinski offers American/Trilateral *superiority*. While trilateralism suggests a more loosely linked set of relations with the Soviet political order, it is not geared to disaggregating and decentralizing the consequences of a major crisis in any area of Soviet-American interaction.

By emphasizing the *bloc* character and power of the West, the Brzezinski image gives added impetus to the Soviet Union's attempts to standardize and insulate its domestic and international political order. In turn, these attempts are likely to lower the threshold for individual East European nationalist responses—precisely the double-edged sword Brzezinski legitimately worries about. The emphasis on hierarchical control and re-compartmentalization increases the likelihood of rash political actions by some ex-colonial and East European countries, like Romania, whose memberships and roles in the international order will depend in Brzezinski's scheme on their ability to establish a client relationship with either the Trilateral organization or the World Socialist System. Brzezinski's image of detente re-emphasizes a stereotypical and invidious status for East European and ex-colonial states, the very states with a growing

---

[21] Brzezinski, p. 121.

[22] Standardization refers to one state's attempt to establish by command an authoritative limit to the permissible range of ideological, institutional, and policy variation within another state. The opposite of standardization would be consensus—i.e., agreement by equals on the limits of change.

concern that the international order be organized so as to allow them to adopt different memberships in different arenas and to have complementary facets to their political identity.

Finally, Brzezinski's emphasis on Western bloc boundaries would logically lead to attempts at a *de facto* American alliance with China, an "understanding" between China and Japan, and the isolation of the Soviet Union. The position of former Defense Secretary Schlesinger thus emerges as the logical outcome of Brzezinski's argument, much as Brzezinski himself might resist such a conclusion.

The danger of a strategy that has as its implicit goal the isolation of the Soviet Union should be manifest. Such a strategy ignores structural change in the global arena—namely, the emergence of the Soviet Union as a global power able to make its presence felt on a continuous basis in all domains. Such a strategy of isolation also fails to appreciate the type of attitude and ethos that accompanied the change in the Soviet international position. Accession to a global status may be assumed to have created within the Soviet elite a heightened sense of pride, and heightened sensitivity to matters of status and prestige. An international strategy that fails to appreciate the structural and subjective changes associated with the Soviet position is a very dangerous strategy.

The risks associated with Kissinger's image of detente lie with the superimposition of conflicts *and the tendency to define all international conflicts as conflicts between the United States and the Soviet Union* (e.g., see Portugal and Angola). The risk associated with Brzezinski's image of detente lies with the failure to accept the consequences of the Soviet rise to global power.

IV. BREZHNEV'S IMAGE OF DETENTE

Brezhnev's image of detente attempts to deal with a structural dilemma and political challenge that confronts the Soviet leadership in a number of arenas.

A fundamental conflict, or the potential for one, exists between the imperatives of hegemony and equality in the relations of the Communist Party of the Soviet Union (CPSU) to the Soviet "citizenry"; in the relationship between the Soviet regime and the party-regimes of Eastern Europe; in the relationship between the Soviet regime and non-communist third world regimes; and in relations between the Soviet Party and non-ruling communist parties (particularly in Western Europe). Any Soviet leadership must face and attempt to resolve this dyad of conflicting imperatives. Brezhnev's image of detente can thus be most fruitfully analyzed as an attempt hegemonically to square the egalitarian circle in each of the above arenas.

Brezhnev must attempt to reconcile the emerging political claims of Soviet citizens for equality with the hegemonical, privileged position of the Party. As he noted in his speech commemorating the fiftieth anniversary of the USSR: "On the basis of the . . . all-round socio-political changes over the past half-century our society has risen to a qualitatively new level. . . . A new historical entity of men—the Soviet people—has been established and has become a reality in this country."[23] This "new reality" is not easily integrated within a political system in which one corporate institution, the Party, maintains its claim to be coextensive with the political order. Such a claim implies political hegemony and domination, not integration.[24] *In identifying itself with the political order, the Party prevents the emergence of a political framework in which Party members and Soviet "citizens" can be equal.*

One section of Brezhnev's speech of the Twenty-Fifth Party Congress suggests that he realizes the crisis potential in the party domination/political integration "fault." In it he pointed to the open, public character of relations between the Party and the Soviet people. His example was the reports of Party personnel to workers on the substance of pre-election Party meetings.[25] His attention to this matter suggests a sensitivity to latent demands within the Soviet population for more equal status with the Party hierarchy. His example also reveals the Party's continued commitment to domination

---

[23] Leonid Brezhnev, *On the Policy of the Soviet Union and the International Situation* (New York: Doubleday and Company, 1973), p. 205.

[24] There are two basic forms of political organization: domination and integration. Domination refers to an organization based *unidimensionally* on the principle of hierarchy. Typically this situation reflects the successful appropriation of exclusive political status by the officials of the organization. The hegemony of this group typically rests on the ideological claim that political membership is an essential, indivisible quality, and on the organizational monopoly of all political roles. Integration refers to an organization based on the conflicting principles of hierarchy and association: to the existence of a *multidimensional* organization in which a membership status such as citizen is distinguishable from that of official—non-official status and has authoritative political weight.

[25] "Report to the XXV Congress (CPSU)," *Foreign Broadcast Information Service*, Sov-76-38, Vol. 3, No. 38, supp. 16 (25 February 1976), p. 47.

of the political system, its intention to maintain the exclusive-esoteric control of the party organization over political life. Consultation with and reports to the "laity"—i.e., the Soviet people—constitute adaptive responses to egalitarian aspirations, not instances of equal membership or participation in the political order.

The Soviet leadership faces comparable problems in other arenas. In Eastern Europe, "loyal" regimes such as the Polish are the equivalent of the new "loyal" Soviet citizen. These regimes are concerned with upgrading their status and with recognition as active, loyal, capable members of the World Socialist System. The Soviet leadership finds it difficult for ideological and practical reasons simply to deny these claims. Yet, this same leadership's conception of its vanguard role in the World Socialist System makes it impossible to grant equal status to other regimes. Within the bloc and domestically, hegemony and equality must be continually juggled in an effort to respond to the latter while maintaining the former.

Outside the context of the Soviet political order the same dilemma confronts the regime. In its relations with third-world regimes the Soviet Union reserves a special role for communist regimes, and especially for the Soviet regime, while proclaiming the unity of all anti-imperialist forces. One of the major sources of conflict between the Soviet and Romanian regimes is the Romanian tendency to ask publicly on what basis "some members" (i.e., the Soviet Union) of the anti-imperialist "coalition" claim special status.

In relations between the CPSU and non-ruling West European communist parties the same sort of conflict exists both in latent and manifest forms. Here the issue revolves around the notion of a "leading center" for the communist parties of the world, which the CPSU implicitly favors, while a growing number of non-ruling parties argue for what amounts to more equality.

Finally, it is plausible to argue that the Soviet leadership aspires to a global hegemonic position. It would be odd for this regime to claim such a position in every other arena and not on the global level. However, one should avoid automatically equating the emergence of the Soviet Union as a global power with its emergence as an imperialist power. Whether it attempts to use its global power imperialistically depends on contingent developments within the Soviet Union, its international bloc, and in the West—particularly on American policy. Having said this, it is important to note that the Soviet Party's organizational character predisposes it to achieve hegemonic status.

Its maintenance of a hegemonic posture towards its own society and the majority of East European regimes and its attempt to secure and enhance this position in the Third World, as well as in relations with non-ruling communist parties, reveal a political order that for all its modern elements remains the most powerful contemporary example of institutionalized charisma along with the Roman Catholic Church.

Brezhnev's image of detente reflects an effort to maintain the Party and regime's charismatic exclusivity as *the* locus of political power and authority within arenas in which an increasing number of actors aspire to, and even demand, equal status. If granted, these demands would involve a fundamental redefinition of the Party's character—its commitments and power. In somewhat different terms the question Brezhnev must resolve is: with the entry and continuous presence of the Soviet regime in a highly diverse set of global and regional arenas, how can the Party and regime maintain and extend their dominance while responding effectively to the range of egalitarian aspirations and demands with which they are increasingly confronted?

Recognizing the impossibility of integrating competing claims of political hegemony and equality, Brezhnev has attempted to shift the terms of debate and conflict from political to economic matters. This strategy depends first of all on his ability to secure agreement from those likely to make equality the defining issue, to deal with it only in social and economic terms; and second, on his ability to isolate those who refuse to accept these terms. Brezhnev favors a strategy of "economism" as a means of bridging and displacing the potential antagonism between his Party and regime's hegemonic claims and the resistance to them inside and outside the Soviet Union.

In the Soviet Union and Eastern Europe consumerism constitutes one major expression of this strategy. In Eastern Europe, the Polish, Hungarian, and Czechoslovak regimes rely heavily on this strategy to maintain political stability. Brezhnev made it clear that consumerism is a political strategy when he pointed out recently that "both the well-being and the *mood of the Soviet people* depend to a large extent on [light industry]."[26] Economic aid to selected East European and Third World regimes is another expression of the sublimation of politics. Finally, Soviet detente policy places a high priority on economic benefits from relations with the United States and Western Europe. Such benefits are seen as providing a critical

---

[26]Brezhnev, "Report to the XXV Congress," p. 42. Emphasis added.

IMAGES OF DETENTE AND THE SOVIET POLITICAL ORDER

base for the Soviet strategy of "economism" domestically and in relations with East European regimes.

Brezhnev appears to see two advantages in this image of detente. First, it works to defuse the potential political crises that run along the hegemony-equality "fault" in the Soviet political order. Second (and here Brezhnev's view parallels Kissinger's), a detente policy that enmeshes the West in a web of commitments to the Soviet Union will reduce the likelihood that one or more Western powers will resort to war against the Soviet Union in order to resolve the "general crisis of capitalism." Kissinger and Brezhnev see each other's domestic and international order as seriously "faulted," and each fears that domestic crises in the other camp will stimulate attempts to solve internal crises through external adventures. Brezhnev's concern that the West might begin to adopt an aggressive stance against the Soviet Union in response to an increasing crisis helps to explain the Soviet leadership's willingness to allow West European communist parties to become part of ruling coalitions on relatively moderate platforms. As members of Western governments these parties, it is hoped, could obstruct any moves towards a "militarist-fascist" policy that would threaten the "stable" development of Soviet domestic and international power.

In other respects Brezhnev's detente policy parallels Brzezinski's more than Kissinger's. Brezhnev would like to see a "trilateral" arrangement of the Soviet Union, Eastern Europe, and Third World regimes that would effectively isolate China and separate Western Europe from the United States. (Similarly, Brzezinski would like to see the Soviet Union isolated, with China and the Soviet Union remaining separated, and the Soviet Union and Eastern Europe becoming separated.)

Brezhnev's image of detente has not, however, gone unchallenged. While there are many sources of opposition to his position, I wish to suggest that Brezhnev has a rather specific interpretation of what the major threat to his strategy is and its source. In Brezhnev's view, the World Socialist System or group of ruling communist regimes has reached a point in its development comparable to that reached by the Soviet regime domestically in the mid-thirties. In both instances (according to Brezhnev) the new order had achieved a relatively dominant but still somewhat fragile position. He has described the internal Soviet situation in the thirties as follows:

> In the 1930's, socialism was firmly established in every sphere of life in our country. . . . Conditions were being created for

the next great stride along the way mapped out by Lenin. *This was prevented by the war.*[27]

More recently Brezhnev has pointed to the gains made by the World Socialist System, particularly in Vietnam, by the East German regime, and through the more effective inclusion of Cuba into the Soviet political order. However, while highly significant, these gains are by no means seen as having irreversible implications for future international development. Rather, Brezhnev appears to see a threat to the political-economic consolidation of the World Socialist System equal in import to the threat that Nazi Germany offered to internal Soviet development in the thirties. In Brezhnev's view, Stalinism with its overriding emphasis on security, vigilance, and extra-legal measures was a distorted development brought about by Nazi Germany's machinations. Today, China appears to threaten Soviet attempts to consolidate a Soviet-led World Socialist System that will stably and relatively peacefully attain global hegemony, much as Germany threatened Soviet domestic development forty years earlier.

What does the Chinese threat consist of? Brezhnev is quite correct that the Chinese challenge the very basis of the current Soviet leadership's attempts to sidestep the hegemony-equality "fault." The Chinese insist on the centrality of the political equality issue in every arena. They point to Russian domination of non-Russian nationalities in the Soviet Union and to the privileged position of the Party apparatus over the Soviet people. They emphasize the threat posed by the neo-colonial, hegemonical claims of the Soviet Union to the sovereignty of East European regimes. The Chinese encourage the Romanians and, thus, provide an example and alternative way of organizing relations with the Soviet Union, which a regime such as the Polish might at some point emulate.

In its addresses to the Third World, China stresses the Soviet attempt to establish a new imperialism and special status in the anti-imperialist coalition. Again, it is the Chinese who warn the Americans and West Europeans that Soviet detente is an insidious route to Soviet international hegemony. By emphasizing political equality and political opposition to Soviet hegemony (or hegemonical claims) as the central issue in all arenas, the Chinese threaten the Brezhnev reformist strategy of sidestepping and displacing the egalitarian challenges, of avoiding hard choices affecting the Soviet Party's and regime's character. From Brezhnev's perspective, by undermining his strategy of detente, the Chinese increase the chance of war in at least

[27] Brezhnev, *On the Policy of the Soviet Union*, p. 24. Emphasis added.

three ways. They do so, first, by encouraging East European nationalism of the Romanian variant; second, by encouraging militarist anti-Soviet actions in the West (through support of figures such as Strauss in West Germany); third, by encouraging a Russian militarist-ethnic reaction in the Soviet Union as a response to the first two developments in East and West Europe.

Brezhnev's comments at the Twenty-Fifth Party Congress reflected his view of the Chinese as the major political threat to his image of detente: he asserted that their attitude was not only incompatible with, but actually hostile to, Marxism-Leninism. China thereby becomes something to be combatted and isolated. Brezhnev's emphasis on "proletarian internationalism"[28] in the same forum may also be taken as indirect evidence that he recognizes the threat posed by the Chinese insistence on *national* equality and sovereignty.

In his efforts to isolate the Chinese and deflect their attempt to articulate international issues in terms of political equality vs. Soviet hegemony, Brezhnev must attend to at least three political actors with particular care: in Eastern Europe, Poland; in Western Europe, the French Communist Party; and in the World Socialist System, Cuba. In these cases, the Soviet regime must square its hegemonic claims with the respective Polish, French, and Cuban claims for a more equal status. In light of the Chinese "threat," Cuba remains a particular source of Soviet uncertainty because of its potential support of the Chinese emphasis on national and party equality. Cuban involvement in the Angolan affair has in some ways increased this uncertainty insofar as Soviet dependence on Cuba's charismatic-revolutionary credentials was one result of this joint venture. (In a comparable fashion Chinese performance in the Korean war made the presentation of claims on the Soviet Union easier.)

Given Castro's charismatic claims, why has he aligned Cuba so closely to the Soviet superpower? There are at least four reasons. The most immediate is Cuban dependence on Soviet economic aid.[29] While this dependence is significant, it does not appear to be the critical factor. There is also the matter of military dependence. Cuba, more than China, remains vulnerable to American intervention. A third and even more important reason is that the Soviet Union owes

---

[28] Brezhnev, "Report to the XXV Congress," p. 11; see p. 26 for comment on proletarian internationalism.

[29] For a recent analysis of Cuban-Soviet relations and internal Cuban developments that relies too heavily on the economic argument see Edward Gonzales, "Castro and Cuba's New Orthodoxy," *Problems of Communism*, Vol. XXV (January-February 1976), pp. 1-19.

any increases in its own revolutionary-charismatic authority to its support of the Cuban engagement of anti-MPLA forces in Angola. However, the major reason for the close alignment of Cuba with the Soviet Union may be Castro's fear that renewed ties with the United States would increase the danger of ideological and cultural contamination. In light of Castro's ability thus far to align with the Soviet Union without visibly sacrificing his personal political power in Cuba[30] he may well see closer ideological and economic coordination with the Soviet bloc as necessary for the ideological-cultural consolidation of his revolution. Cuban alignment depends on Castro's seeing no real domestic threat to his dominant position and on future evidence of Soviet support for Angolan type situations. The latter is the Achilles heel of the relationship. Basically, Angola was an instance of Soviet inability to do anything but support the Cubans. Soviet and Cuban interests in national liberation wars are not totally dissimilar; but they are dissimilar enough to be the source of future conflict.

Soviet behavior in Western Europe can also be explained in terms of Brezhnev's desire to deflect the Chinese attempt to define international issues in terms of national equality. This desire helps to explain the conflicting positions taken by the Soviet regime and the French Communist Party (PCF) at the time of the May 1974 elections: the Soviet ambassador paid a visit to Giscard d'Estaing, a visit that could well have been delayed until after the second ballot; the PCF Politburo called the Soviet initiative "regrettable."[31]

One explanation of this behavior might be that it was a Soviet attempt to cover all bets. Should Giscard win, as he did, the Soviet leadership would not have placed itself in a position that would facilitate the development of an anti-Soviet, anti-detente policy in France. Should the PCF coalition win, the presence of the PCF in the government would work against Chinese efforts to unite West Europe in a nationalist reaction against the Soviet Union. For all the real conflict between the Soviet regime and the PCF over the

---

[30] For evidence of this see *ibid.*, pp. 14-18.

[31] See Ronald Tiersky, "The French Communist Party and Detente," *Journal of International Affairs*, Vol. 28 (1974), pp. 188-206. See the same author's "French Communism in 1976," *Problems of Communism*, Vol. XXV (January-February 1976), pp. 20-46.

For a comprehensive and valuable survey and analysis of West European parties see Neil McInnes, *The Communist Parties of Western Europe* (New York: Oxford University Press, 1975), in particular the chapter on "The Communists and Neo-capitalist Democracy," pp. 160-207.

election, both had and still have a basic interest in the continuation of Brezhnev's policy of detente.

That policy is threatened not only directly by the Chinese but also indirectly by the possible emergence of a leadership faction within the Soviet regime emphasizing ethnic-military policies in response to the Chinese "threat," and particularly in response to the degree of international success the Chinese may achieve. This appears to be one of Brezhnev's major concerns and a quite legitimate one.

Domestic opposition to Brezhnev's image of detente and his domestic policy is suggested by disputes currently centering on the attempt to write a new Soviet Constitution. This endeavor seems to be the locus for a wide-ranging set of disputes and policy issues central to the future organization and ideological definition of the Soviet political order.

It would appear that in response to this opposition and in order to guarantee continuity to his image of detente, Brezhnev has taken steps to encourage a stable succession after his retirement, one that will insure continued conformity to the basic outlines of his policy for Soviet national and international development.

Two developments in particular can be explained in these terms. First, the Party Secretariat has increased its relative political weight. Second, there has been a pronounced tendency to recruit individuals from the same age group (around 60 years of age) to fill a large number of critical institutional posts. These moves can be interpreted as a conscious and adaptive response to the problem of succession within a charismatic institution that refuses to regulate its actions by means of a legal-political framework separate from the Party framework. Selection of an elite cadre within a narrow age range, with shared experiences, and possibly with a notable degree of personal ties and ease in communication, together with a narrowing of the actual number of decision-makers, looks like a deliberate political maneuver designed to provide at least minimal stability and continuity after Brezhnev's withdrawal.

Recent Soviet efforts to achieve greater political and ideological standardization in Eastern Europe parallel the internal Soviet attempts to insure stability and continuity. Brezhnev's efforts reflect a continuing Soviet commitment to a charismatic (i.e., vanguard) conception of leadership and membership. This conception favors a political order based on hegemony not equality, and on domination rather than integration. Development towards political equality in any part of the Soviet political order will only occur in spite of Party preferences, not because of them.

V. EASTERN EUROPE, WESTERN EUROPE, AND DETENTE

The significance of Eastern Europe as an area directly affected by American and Soviet conceptions and policies was dramatically demonstrated in the second debate between the two American presidential candidates of 1976. Their respective confusion over Eastern Europe was more revealing than their expressed concern. For Ford, the fact that Poland, Romania, and Yugoslavia (as well as Albania) enjoy a more autonomous status vis-a-vis the Soviet Union than East Germany, Bulgaria, Hungary, and Czechoslovakia meant that Eastern Europe is no longer dominated by the Soviet Union. However, of equal importance is the fact that this autonomy exists without the concomitant ideological acceptance by the Soviets of state sovereignty as the fundamental characteristic of international relations.[32] Thus the existence of some regime autonomy in East Europe is evidence of Soviet pragmatism rather than of ideological change. For this reason it is correct to argue that such autonomy as does exist in the area is highly unstable.

Carter, on the other hand, was unable to recognize those differences in political status that do exist. And both men failed to indicate any appreciation of the relationship that exists between the type of detente policy America adopts and (a) the ease or difficulty with which the Soviet Union implements different patterns of control in Eastern Europe; (b) the success or failure of different Eastern European regimes in extending the scope and stability of their autonomous positions; and (c) the potential for violent encounters in Soviet-Eastern European relations.

Certainly, all the images of detente that we have analyzed severely limit the ability of Soviet-bloc regimes to adopt complementary rather than mutually exclusive political memberships, policies, and identities. Each image of detente here examined favors a hierarchical and compartmentalized international order, whether in the form of an Atlantic Alliance, Trilateral Commission, or World Socialist System.

The Kissinger strategy of enmeshment, part of which seems to involve closer relations between the Soviet Union and Eastern Europe, favors a situation in which domestic Soviet conflicts be-

---

[32] In fact the Brezhnev Doctrine is not an innovation. In 1958, ten years earlier, Alexei Rumiantsev, the editor of *World Marxist Review*, noted that the "qualitatively new forms of relations ... [among] the socialist countries ... are not limited to a recognition of equality and sovereignty." (See Alexander Dallin, ed., *Diversity in International Communism* [New York, 1963], p. 624.)

tween Russians and non-Russians, and between the Party and the Soviet "citizenry," will be *superimposed* on the "faults" that characterize regime-society relations in Eastern European countries and Soviet-Eastern European regime relations. In these circumstances if a crisis should occur anywhere in the Soviet political order, the most likely response in Eastern Europe would be intense nationalism as the only available means of protective decoupling. Should such a development occur in Poland, the consequences for peace in Europe would be very serious.

The Brzezinski Trilateral-"bridge-building" combination also limits East European political choices. Trilateralism *cum* "bridge-building" seeks simultaneously to strengthen the Western bloc and to pry loose East European regimes from Leninism. If anything, this policy would strengthen Soviet efforts to increase its bloc's organizational cohesion (i.e., Soviet hierarchical power) and political uniformity. Kissinger's, Brzezinski's, and Brezhnev's images of detente all work to limit the options available to East European regimes. Western and Soviet emphasis on hierarchical and relatively compartmentalized definitions of international relations present only two choices to any East European regime that acts to expand its political memberships, policies, and autonomy. One choice—the Polish—is co-optation by the Soviets in return for a higher status[33] and policy maneuverability *within the framework of Soviet hegemony*; the other—the Romanian—is adoption of a nationalist position in an effort to assert national equality and the consequent right to adopt a set of complementary memberships, policies, and self-conceptions.

The first route risks jeopardizing the domestic stability of an East European country by the regime's apparent dependence on the Soviet Union—e.g., the recent crises over the revision of the Polish constitution. The risk is enhanced by the danger that the Soviet regime will not adequately take the foreign leadership's problems into account when pursuing Soviet interests. The second choice risks both Soviet invasion and exclusion of that regime from bloc affairs.

A similarly narrow set of choices exists for non-East European communist actors in their relations with the Soviet regime. Among non-ruling parties the French occupy a "Polish" position, while the Italians (and even more so the Spanish) occupy a "Romanian"

---

[33] While only an impression, it appears to me that Poland has been granted something of a junior executive status by the Soviet elite in the organization of the Soviet bloc. The Polish leadership has been given preferential status at the symbolic level and very likely has been awarded a special role of sorts in the context of Soviet-East European relations.

position. Within the World Socialist System, Cuba (currently) occupies a "Polish" position, while China's position resembles more the "Romanian."

Political choices for East European regimes are limited by the Soviet commitment to a hierarchical, centrally managed, compartmentalized political division of labor. In turn, this stereotypic Soviet image of international relations is supported by the preference of Western leaders for a detente based on similar premises.[34]

The result is that an attempt by an East European regime to complicate its identity, to claim the right and capacity to play different political roles in different international settings, must remain a high-risk venture, as it was for Hungary in 1956, for Czechoslovakia in 1968, and to a lesser degree for Romania in recent years. *Increased policy choice within the framework of an exclusive identity (i.e., bloc and communist) is possible, while an increased capacity to adopt complementary memberships remains highly risky.*[35]

A brief examination of the Romanian case might serve to illustrate some of these points more sharply. Whereas earlier Romania's political self-conception and policies were hierarchically oriented (i.e., defined in terms of Soviet interests), in recent years it has differentiated its political identity and adopted a more diverse and complementary set of political references, memberships, and policies. At present, Romania defines itself not simply as a socialist state, but also as a small state, a European nation, and an ex-colonial polity.[36] Its foreign policies reflect these differentiations. However, because Romania acts in an international setting influenced by two superpowers who agree basically on the need to structure international life on the principles of centralization and compartmentalization, the Romanian political effort at diversification is continually

[34]To argue that most Western conceptions of detente are predicated on premises similar to those held by the Soviet elite (i.e., hierarchy and compartmentalization) is not to argue that those in the West committed to these premises favor continued Soviet domination over Eastern Europe. On the other hand, it should be pointed out again that operating with such premises works against ending that domination.

[35]The most recent, thorough, and informed statement on Soviet-East European relations is in J.F. Brown, *Relations Between the Soviet Union and Its Eastern European Allies: A Survey* (Santa Monica: Rand Corp., November 1975 [R1742-Pr]).

[36]For an analysis of this development from the perspective of an expansion in political references, memberships, and self-conceptions see the author's contribution in Sylva Sinanian, I. Deak, and P.C. Ludz, eds., *Eastern Europe in the 1970's* (New York: Praeger Publishers, 1972), pp. 180-84.

threatened from two directions. There is, first, the danger of Soviet invasion or of Romania's exclusion from some arenas in which it wishes to be active. Second, and equally serious, is the likelihood that intense ethnic nationalism could become the *only* expression available to the deviant state actor challenging an international system based on hierarchy and compartmentalization.

VI. PROPOSED WESTERN POLICY CHANGES

Given a continued Soviet commitment to a stereotyped international system, what type of detente could the West offer that would (a) recognize the unique power of the Soviet Union and the United States, (b) extend beyond bilateral ties, (c) favor the adoption of more diverse political identities by East European regimes, without immediately threatening them with Soviet invasion or their exclusion from bloc affairs, and (d) strengthen West Europe? U.S. policy to these ends, in contrast to existing images and strategies of detente, should seek to decouple and decentralize issues and geographic areas. Stanley Hoffman has made a similar suggestion in his call for an American policy of "modesty and devolution."[37]

The strategic locus of such a strategy is American-West European relations. *A major condition for East European diversification, for development beyond the mutually exclusive choice between a dangerous degree of nationalism or intensified political dependence, is greater West European diversification and autonomy.* This would include participation of Western communist parties at times in ruling coalitions, and the consequent political integration of significant sectors of the West European working class into national membership status.

In *Alternative to Partition*, Zbigniew Brzezinski declares that "for most of the postwar period the United States has had no real policy for East Europe."[38] On the contrary, our policy towards the area has been a function of our West European policy. Greater West European initiatives, diversification of groupings within and outside the Common Market, and the entry of communist parties into coalition governments could provide incentives and opportunities for more varied forms of West European/East European interaction.

[37] Hoffman, p. 42.
[38] Brzezinski, p. 116.

As for the participation of Western communist parties in ruling coalitions, the behavior of these parties will be constrained by electoral considerations, by the increasing weight of their parliamentary wings, and ultimately by the political and military forces that suspect, scrutinize, and oppose them. West European regimes with communist participation would be more attractive to East European regimes as potential partners in joint efforts and could provide East Europe with a counterweight to its Soviet connection. In addition, the Soviet regime would find it much more difficult to prohibit the emergence of varied organizational arrangements between East and West European regimes under conditions of increased West European autonomy and political diversification inside and outside the Common Market.

One likely criticism of this line of argument might be: "Why give up so much unilaterally to the Soviet Union without their making comparable concessions?" But what exactly would the West be giving up? Participation of the Italian or French communist parties would mean the integration of sizable portions of the Italian and French working classes into their national polities, the ending of their political exclusion and categoric status as "workers." Such a development could strengthen a West Europe currently weakened by social malintegration. Indeed, such a development might provide the base for a more self-confident, assertive, and innovative West Europe in place of one characterized by major social cleavages and an inability to translate economic and political potential into economic and political power. Furthermore, what other choices does the United States have? Continuing to deal with West Europe as though it were 1956, as though major changes have not occurred within this area, can only bring about further crises within the Western world and favor reliance on force rather than politics as the means of resolving those crises.

A detente strategy of decoupling assumes three things: (a) That the global power of the United States and the Soviet Union will remain the primary fact of international relations for a very long time. It assumes that attempts to establish more disaggregated, decentralized, cross-cutting, political and economic relationships, each claiming only part of a state's political identity, can shape the use of that global power with fewer risks and greater benefits more evenly distributed.

(b) That West European countries are politically capable of allowing communist participation in coalitions without succumbing to communist efforts to subvert the democratic order and establish a position of political hegemony. In light of the Portuguese experience and American global-nuclear power, one would think that France, Italy, or Spain could manage as well as Portugal, Finland, and Iceland.

(c) That the United States and Western Europe will be able to maintain regular, close, effective ties of a political, economic, cultural, and military nature in the absence of NATO and in the presence of a more diversified set of West European groupings.

The goal of such a detente policy would be the development of an international structure that would allow East European and West European regimes, and others, to adopt multiple points of reference and membership. In contrast to detente based on either indivisibility or compartmentalization, our image favors the proliferation of new political categories, the development of multiple memberships and commitments in the context of two global powers flexibly and reciprocally linked to states of lesser power.

About the author

Kenneth Jowitt is Associate Professor of Political Science at the University of California, Berkeley. His major interests are in the fields of comparative/international politics. He has published works on political organization and development in communist countries, strategies of national development, the international organization of communist regimes, and is currently working on the issue of political membership in industrial and non-industrial societies.

INSTITUTE OF INTERNATIONAL STUDIES
UNIVERSITY OF CALIFORNIA, BERKELEY

CARL G. ROSBERG,
Director

Monographs published by the Institute include:

RESEARCH SERIES

1. *The Chinese Anarchist Movement*, by Robert A. Scalapino and George T. Yu. ($1.00)
3. *Land Tenure and Taxation in Nepal*, Volume I, *The State as Landlord: Raikar Tenure*, by Mahesh C. Regmi. ($8.75; unbound photocopy)
4. *Land Tenure and Taxation in Nepal*, Volume II, *The Land Grant System: Birta Tenure*, by Mahesh C. Regmi. ($2.50)
*5. *Mexico and Latin American Economic Integration*, by Philippe C. Schmitter and Ernst B. Haas. ($1.00)
6. *Local Taxation in Tanganyika*, by Eugene C. Lee. ($1.00)
7. *Birth Rates in Latin America: New Estimates of Historical Trends*, by O. Andrew Collver. ($2.50)
8. *Land Tenure and Taxation in Nepal*, Volume III, *The Jagir, Rakam, and Kipat Tenure Systems*, by Mahesh C. Regmi. ($2.50)
9. *Ecology and Economic Development in Tropical Africa*, edited by David Brokensha. ($8.25; unbound photocopy)
10. *Urban Areas in Indonesia: Administrative and Census Concepts*, by Pauline Dublin Milone. ($10.50; unbound photocopy)
12. *Land Tenure and Taxation in Nepal*, Volume IV, *Religious and Charitable Land Endowments: Guthi Tenure*, by Mahesh C. Regmi. ($2.75)
13. *The Pink Yo-Yo: Occupational Mobility in Belgrade, ca. 1915-1965*, by Eugene A. Hammel. ($2.00)
14. *Community Development in Israel and the Netherlands: A Comparative Analysis*, by Ralph M. Kramer. ($2.50)
*15. *Central American Economic Integration: The Politics of Unequal Benefits*, by Stuart I. Fagan. ($2.00)
16. *The International Imperatives of Technology: Technological Development and the International Political System*, by Eugene B. Skolnikoff. ($2.95)
*17. *Autonomy or Dependence as Regional Integration Outcomes: Central America*, by Philippe C. Schmitter. ($1.75)
18. *Framework for a General Theory of Cognition and Choice*, by Robert M. Axelrod. ($1.50)
19. *Entry of New Competitors in Yugoslav Market Socialism*, by Stephen R. Sacks. ($2.50)
*20. *Political Integration in French-Speaking Africa*, by Abdul A. Jalloh. ($3.50)
21. *The Desert and the Sown: Nomads in the Wider Society*, edited by Cynthia Nelson. ($3.50)
22. *U. S.-Japanese Competition in International Markets: A Study of the Trade-Investment Cycle in Modern Capitalism*, by John E. Roemer. ($3.95)
23. *Political Disaffection Among British University Students: Concepts, Measurement, and Causes*, by Jack Citrin and David J. Elkins. ($2.00)
24. *Urban Inequality and Housing Policy in Tanzania: The Problem of Squatting*, by Richard E. Stren. ($2.50)
*25. *The Obsolescence of Regional Integration Theory*, by Ernst B. Haas. ($2.95)

*International Integration Series

INSTITUTE OF INTERNATIONAL STUDIES MONOGRAPHS (continued)

26. *The Voluntary Service Agency in Israel*, by Ralph M. Kramer. ($2.00)
27. *The SOCSIM Demographic-Sociological Microsimulation Program: Operating Manual*, by Eugene A. Hammel et al. ($4.50)
28. *Authoritarian Politics in Communist Europe: Uniformity & Diversity in One-Party States*, edited by Andrew C. Janos. ($3.75)
29. *The Anglo-Icelandic Cod War of 1972-1973: A Case Study of a Fishery Dispute*, by Jeffrey A. Hart. ($2.00)
30. *Plural Societies and New States: A Conceptual Analysis*, by Robert Jackson. ($2.00)
31. *The Politics of Crude Oil Pricing in the Middle East, 1970-1975: A Study in International Bargaining*, by Richard Chadbourn Weisberg. ($3.50)
32. *Agricultural Policy and Performance in Zambia: History, Prospects, and Proposals for Change*, by Doris Jansen Dodge. ($4.95)

POLITICS OF MODERNIZATION SERIES

1. *Spanish Bureaucratic-Patrimonialism in America*, by Magali Sarfatti. ($2.00)
2. *Civil-Military Relations in Argentina, Chile, and Peru*, by Liisa North. ($2.00)
3. *Notes on the Process of Industrialization in Argentina, Chile, and Peru*, by Alcira Leiserson. ($1.75)
4. *Chilean Christian Democracy: Politics and Social Forces*, by James Petras. ($1.50)
5. *Social Stratification in Peru*, by Magali Sarfatti Larson and Arlene Eisen Bergman. ($4.95)
6. *Modernization and Coercion*, by Mario Barrera. ($1.50)
7. *Latin America: The Hegemonic Crisis and the Military Coup*, by José Nun. ($2.00)
8. *Development Processes in Chilean Local Government*, by Peter S. Cleaves. ($1.50)
9. *Modernization and Bureaucratic-Authoritarianism: Studies in South American Politics*, by Guillermo A. O'Donnell. ($3.50)

WORKING PAPERS ON DEVELOPMENT

1. *Indian Economic Policy and Performance: A Framework for a Progressive Society*, by Jagdish N. Bhagwati. ($1.00)
2. *Toward a Comparative Study of Revolutions*, by Elbaki Hermassi. ($1.50)
3. *Patrons, Clients, and Politicians: New Perspectives on Political Clientelism*, by Keith R. Legg. ($2.00)

POLICY PAPERS IN INTERNATIONAL AFFAIRS

1. *Images of Detente and the Soviet Political Order*, by Kenneth Jowitt. ($1.00)
2. *Detente After Brezhnev: The Domestic Roots of Soviet Foreign Policy*, by Alexander Yanov. ($3.00)
3. *The Mature Neighbor Policy: A New United States Economic Policy for Latin America*, by Albert Fishlow. ($2.00)

Address correspondence to:
Institute of International Studies
215 Moses Hall
University of California
Berkeley, California 94720

LIBRARY OF DAVIDSON COLLEGE

Books on regular loan may be checked out for **two weeks**. Books must be presented at the Circulation Desk in order to be renewed.

A fine is charged after date due.

Special books are subject to special regulations at the discretion of the library staff.

FEB. 12.1979			
SEP 27 1982			